Making Music

by Natalie Goldstein

PEARSON

Scott
Foresman

What You Already Know

Force is a push or pull that can move things. There are different kinds of force.

You push a sled to make it move. Your push is a force. You use force to throw a ball. The force of gravity makes the ball fall to the ground. Gravity pulls things toward the ground.

You throw a ball with a lot of force. It moves fast. You throw a ball with less force. It moves slowly. Speed is how quickly or slowly something moves.

Things move in different ways. Things can move up and down. Things can move right to left. Other things move in a straight line, a curve, or a zigzag. Things can be in different places.

A magnet makes some metal things move. A magnet has a north pole and a south pole. Poles that are different attract each other. Attract means to pull toward. Poles that are the same repel each other. Repel means to push away.

When a sound is made something vibrates. Vibrate means to move back and forth very fast. When you hit a drum, the force makes it vibrate. The vibrating drum makes sound.

Sounds are all around. People make sounds. Nature makes sounds. You will read how musical sounds are made.

Sound and Music

When something vibrates, the air around it vibrates too. The vibration moves through the air. You hear sound when the vibration gets to your ears.

Instruments vibrate to make sounds. A musical sound is called a note.

Different musical instruments make different sounds that we can hear.

**Sound vibrations move through the air.
This makes the grains of rice jump.**

Blowing air into a recorder makes vibrations. Tapping piano keys makes vibrations too. Hitting a pot makes it vibrate like a drum.

Different musical instruments make the air vibrate differently. So different instruments make different sounds.

Percussion

Some instruments make sound when you hit or shake them. These are percussion instruments.

A xylophone (ZEYE-luh-fohn) has bars. Tapping the bars with a stick makes the bars vibrate. Different bars make different sounds.

Xylophone

Tambourine

Drum

Tambourines and drums vibrate when they are hit. Maracas vibrate when the seeds inside them move.

Notes start and stop at different times. This is called a rhythm (RITH-uhm). Hit a drum. BOOM ba ba BOOM! The drum plays the rhythm.

Maracas

Blowing Notes

You blow air into some instruments. The air vibrates inside the instrument. The vibrations make sound.

Bottles that have a little water inside also have lots of air inside. Blowing into them makes the air vibrate. Low sounds happen. What kind of sounds happen when you blow into a bottle with lots of water?

Harmonica

Bassoon

Oboe

Instruments you blow into are called wind instruments. A recorder is a wind instrument. Blow into a recorder. The air inside vibrates. A recorder has small holes on one side. Covering different holes changes how the air inside vibrates. It makes different musical notes.

Recorder

Brass instruments are different sizes. Long brass instruments make lower sounds. Many brass instruments have curves. Curves make it easy to hold the instrument.

Some brass instruments have keys to press. Some have a slide that moves. Keys and slides help change notes.

Trumpet

Tuba

Trombone

Strings and Things

Some instruments have strings to pluck, or pull. The strings vibrate. This makes the air inside the instrument move. Sound is made.

A guitar (gi-TAR) may have six strings. Thin strings make high notes. Thick strings make low notes.

Guitar

Harp

Cello

Violin

A violin (veye-uh-LIN) is a
string instrument. A bow moves
the strings. The air inside the
instrument vibrates.

Fingers press the strings down
as the bow moves. Pressing different
strings makes different notes.

There are strings inside a piano.

Strings

Keys

A cello (CHEL-oh) is like a big violin. It has longer and thicker strings than a violin. A cello makes lower notes than a violin.

There are strings inside a piano. Near each string is a tiny hammer. Tap a piano key. One hammer moves. It hits one string. The string vibrates and makes a note.

Playing Together

All musical sounds are made by vibrating air. Vibrations in musical instruments, water bottles, and singing voices all make sounds.

Cymbals

Clarinet

Violin

A little air vibrating makes a different sound than a lot of air vibrating. Different instruments vibrate in different ways. This is why instruments make different musical sounds. Together, the sounds can make many kinds of music.

French horn

Cello

Glossary

instrument   something that makes music

musical   having to do with music

note   a musical sound

pluck   to pick or pull

rhythm   the way notes start and stop

sound   what happens when vibrating air reaches someone's ears

vibration   fast movement back and forth